This Book Belongs to:

_____

_____

_____

- I am a leader.

I Am Energy!

The Super Hero Edition

Written & Illustrated by: Maria Moon

il♥veloni
www.iloveloni.com

Energy is everything.
Energy is me.
The table, The T. V, the grass at my feet

Energy is everywhere.
So small I can't see.
Vibrating fast, quick as lightning.

Energy makes up all things.
Energy makes me.
Can I touch energy if it's something I can't see

We can't touch energy itself,
Because it isn't a thing.
is a force, a power, a special type of strength.

You don't have to touch it to know it's there
You can feel, hear & smell the magic in the ai

ke the silent hummmmm from the refrigerator.
ENERGY!

The snoring Z's from the sleeping Alligator.

ENERGY!

When we go up and down the elevator.
ENERGY!

How about when the phone rings? ENERGY!

Anytime we blink or breathe. ENERGY!

Getting strong from the food we eat.
ENERGY!

The Sun growing the plants and trees.
ENERGY!

When the moon appears for us to sleep
ENERGY!

The stars dance to their own beat.
ENERGY!

See, Energy is in everything.
Think of energy as a battery you can't see.
It makes the world go around.
It makes you and me!